T0194958

Miracles UNFOLDING

Shelley Thody

WESTBOW
PRESS®
A DIVISION OF THOMAS NELSON
& ZONDERVAN

WestBow Press books may be ordered through
booksellers or by contacting:

WestBow Press
A Division of Thomas Nelson & Zondervan
1663 Liberty Drive
Bloomington, IN 47403
www.westbowpress.com
844-714-3454

Scripture quotations taken from The Holy Bible, New International
Version® NIV® Copyright © 1973 1978 1984 2011 by Biblica, Inc.
TM. Used by permission. All rights reserved worldwide.

Scriptures and additional materials quoted are from the
Good News Bible © 1994 published by the Bible Societies/
HarperCollins Publishers Ltd UK, Good News Bible© American
Bible Society 1966, 1971, 1976, 1992. Used with permission.

ISBN: 978-1-6642-3929-6 (sc)
ISBN: 978-1-6642-3928-9 (e)

Library of Congress Control Number: 2021913273

Print information available on the last page.

WestBow Press rev. date: 7/8/2021

Contents

I dedicate this work to the Indigenous People
of Canada, many of whom are my neighbours,
friends, colleagues, Christian brothers
and sisters and students. May the terrible
and tragic wounds of so many be healed
through God's truth and unfailing love.

"Every Child Matters"

Introduction

After completing my first book, I felt relief and hope that my story about bipolar disorder might help someone else struggling with such a debilitating mental health disorder. I was praying my story could provide some hope. However, during the publishing process, fear started to creep in. I put my darkest, most disturbing self in the text for all to read and judge. There were neighbors, parents, coworkers, family and community members who would read my words. I was feeling vulnerable. What if I lost my job? What if my husband lost his? What if my children were bullied? I started sinking in the water. My faith was being tested. Instead of letting these feelings and questions take hold of me, I prayed a great deal and kept forging ahead. I was convinced Satan did not want my book out in the public, but I believed God did! Thankfully, my convictions overruled these doubts, due to my faith in Jesus.

> **"Do not be afraid of them. Your God, the Lord himself will lead you and be with you. He will not fail you or abandon you, so do not lose courage or be afraid." (Deuteronomy 31:6) GNB**

In early 2013, I had my published book in hand, and once again God's grace was evident in my life. He had protected me and my family from harm coming from the release of my book. Any of the fears I harboured were negated by the awesome, positive response of countless people. Wonderful conversations with many readers led to revelations about people they loved dealing with mental health disorders. Some readers even felt comfortable sharing their own mental health struggles with me. My children were not negatively affected or bullied at all. Our jobs were secure and there was an incredible, supportive response from friends, parents, coworkers, community and even strangers. My fears were not necessary. God had this. God protected me as the following song describes so vividly, with one line stating: "Hallelujah, great defender, so much better Your way." **"Defender"** by Francesca Battistelli and Stefany Gretzinger

Not only did God protect me from possible threats ensuing from the candidness of my book, detailing my debilitating symptoms from long ago, He also gifted me and my family with many incredible things since the book was written. How could I not share these wonderful miracles which have solidified my faith, so others might be inspired to believe in Jesus or deepen their confidence in Him.

Preface

We live in a world of constant change and uncertainty. I have known this fact for most of my life. However, 2020 brought such abundant change and uncertainty we often longed for a sense of normalcy. Because of Covid-19, the world as we knew it is so very different. Lately, many of us have been uncertain about our health, jobs, flights, vacations, places to live, or even having food on our plate on a daily basis. It has been extremely difficult for almost everyone and much harder on certain people than on others.

My family and I have dealt with incredible changes since the middle of March, 2020 when the pandemic hit. I suddenly went from teaching children in real life to attempting to educate them over a computer. I teach grade three students and I am *not* computer savvy. Our daughters both made their way back home from other areas in Alberta; Kristy from the nursing program in Fort McMurray and Jamilyn from Calgary, where she just finished her degree. My son Jesse in grade 11 was suddenly learning from home on the computer and his hockey was cancelled, both great disappointments in his final years of high school. One constant was my husband Dale who continued to be of service to our community through his job as a plumber. His only change during the pandemic was my persistent harping to wash his hands and use hand sanitizer.

In the midst of all of these changes were the constant reminders of the number of Covid-19 cases, how to stay safe, cancellations, places closing down, flights cancelled...and worst of all, the increasing deaths around the world. We were always being reminded to social-distance, self-isolate, sneeze in our sleeves and wash our hands often. Many people were incredibly lonely. The fact we are mortal human beings was suddenly at the forefront of our lives. Everyone was frequently reminded we are not at the wheel and we are not in control, causing many to feel a great deal of fear and uncertainty in the world.

Where was our normal? Where was our predictability? Where was our peace?

The only trustworthy constant I have ever known, or ever will know is Jesus. He is my true companion in a world that is so incredibly unpredictable. He is my peace and my hope and my salvation. I serve a living God. The stories I have to share of miracles unfolding are recent. I felt God compelling me to share this good news when our world is experiencing such a hard and difficult time, to remind us our hope is in Jesus.

Chapter 1

MELANCHOLY, MANIA AND MIRACLES

My first book written between 2010 and 2012 was titled *Melancholy, Mania and Miracles*. I was diagnosed with Bipolar Disorder when I was 19 years old, and the book is based on my three year roller-coaster ride of highs and lows, progressing to the highest of highs—a sense of euphoria, very little sleep and grandiose notions of myself—and the lowest of lows. What goes up must inevitably come down, and life most certainly came crashing down on me. This led to my extreme depression and attempted suicide in 1987.

One of the many miracles in this story starts with God's great grace in saving me physically from my attempt to take my own life. I almost died on the gurney twice before paramedics could start driving me to the hospital. My dad and my sister had to watch this horror unfold. Ultimately, the outcome was God's decision. He saved me from death and darkness. He had a plan for me. He pulled me back into life through His grace and the love from my beautiful family. He had a plan for my eternal salvation.

Despite everything I put my family through years before, especially my mom, Dale and I were blessed with a miracle through the birth of our first child. Jamilyn was born ten years after the dreadful time of my extreme mental health challenges when I came so close to dying. Children are miracles from heaven. God forgiving my sins and providing me with such a blessing, was truly incredible. Jamilyn was born on my mom's birthday. What a blessing! She was a true gift from God to Dale, myself, and my mom, with timing only He could have planned.

Another miracle mentioned in my first book occurred six years later. Dale and I were extremely satisfied having had two beautiful daughters. Life was busy. I was thankful for the blessings of our girls and my step-daughter Kayla. After a great deal of discussion, we decided Dale was going to have a vasectomy. He went into the hospital in our town and was operated on by one of our leading doctors with a great reputation. Dale healed with minimal pain and a few ice packs. A couple of months later, another assessment was done to determine if any sperm was still present. Our doctor soon called us back to say he felt that Dale should have another operation as he noticed that the sperm count was low, but still present.

Reluctantly, Dale prepped for yet another vasectomy procedure. I dropped him off at the hospital and went home to be with the girls. A short time later, I surprisingly received a call to pick Dale up. The doctor had changed his mind about the second operation after consulting another urologist. The specialist concluded the procedure was not necessary. He said, "Don't worry about such a little amount of sperm count. Pregnancy would be virtually impossible with such a low count." Eight months later I was looking at a positive pregnancy test and I couldn't believe it! Was this really correct? Apparently it was, and several months later our son Jesse Rhys arrived. Wow! How our life changed. The impossible is possible with God. Dale and I had been blessed with our *only son.* God most certainly had a plan. He knew how much Dale and I needed this boy in our lives. More importantly, how He needed Jesse in this world.

At this point in my life, I began to think about God and his power a great deal. I knew after what I had been through, God was leading me to wonderful things I felt I didn't deserve. I couldn't have stabilized my bipolar, gone on to work, achieved my Bachelor of Education degree, gotten married and received three beautiful children on my own. Especially after the tumultuous mental health disorder I had been dealing with. I still hadn't committed my life to the Lord at this point, although I was definitely seeking and offering an abundance of thanks.

> *"Be confident, my heart, because the Lord has been good to me. The Lord saved me from death; he stopped my tears and kept me from defeat. And so I walk in the presence of the Lord."* **(Psalm 116:7-9) GNB**

Since the birth of our children, the Lord has blessed us with a great deal of gifts, including living in the community of Lac La Biche. We have a lovely home, a wonderful church family, twenty five years of stable employment, three grandchildren from Kayla and Billy, and an abundance of hope. Looking back into the darkness of over thirty years ago and comparing that time to where I am now, how could I not rejoice? I share in celebration of what our beautiful Saviour and some of His unfolding miracles have done, in my life alone.

Faith in Jesus can lead to amazing outcomes in our lives. I believe the following miracles I am about to share with you are a result of my close and trusting relationship with the Lord and His protection over me. I listened to His calling to share my mental health story. I trusted in Him, not myself. God's faithfulness and love for us is amazing!

> *"So whether you eat or drink, or whatever you do, do it all for the glory of God."* **(1 Corinthians 10:31) NIV**

Chapter 2

THE POWER OF PRAYER

During the time between completing my book and awaiting publishing, I suffered from a difficult depression for over two weeks. In retrospect, I believe it was an attack from Satan who most definitely did not want the book to succeed. I felt very defeated. I was able to go to work through this time, but I couldn't muster enough energy at home to barely smile or spend much time with my family. There was a constant flow of tears.

My husband was acutely aware of my depression and filled in the gaps where I couldn't. Dale had also been suffering with the discomfort of scoliosis for over thirty years. He had constant pain in his lower back that became excruciating at times. He said it often felt like a knife being stuck in his back. He rarely ever complained about the pain, but I could always see in his actions and facial expressions when it was bad. Dale found sitting very difficult and could only lay on his back to sleep. To complicate the matter even more, he worked physically demanding jobs all of his life. Dale would take the odd ibuprofen to ease some of the pain, but he was told by doctors there was little he could do for his scoliosis.

One night, closer to the end of my two week depression, Dale was suddenly awakened with an intense burning feeling in his lower back. Very unselfishly, and through the pain, he put his arm around me and said a prayer for *me*. As he was praying for my depression to be healed, he felt an incredibly hot sensation in his lower back. As the heat dissipated, so did his back pain. He moved around and he couldn't feel any more pain...*at all*.

Dale revealed this miraculous event to me a couple of days later when he saw a smile touch my face once again. I couldn't believe it. I was feeling so much better and Dale had no more pain in his back. How could this be? I already felt confident I knew the answer. This was an amazing gift from God! We were so incredibly blessed and thankful. Quite honestly though, we wondered if it was temporary relief or more permanent. We have realized the answer to this question as time unfolds. Dale said this prayer and he was healed from his pain on January 30, 2012...over eight years now!

There is a song that I love so much called "**Chain Breaker**" by Zach Williams. It says: if you've got pain, He's a pain taker/ If you've got chains, He's a chain breaker. This song speaks directly to the experience that both of us were going through at this time. God took Dale's physical pain and broke the chains of my mental pain. What an *incredible* God.

With Dale being so grateful and healthier physically, and my depression dissolved for the time being, my first book was soon on the shelves. I was so thankful.

After Dale's selfless prayer for me and my mental illness, I did suffer some short bouts of depression periodically for the next year or two. These episodes only lasted for a few days. Today, I can gratefully state I have not been depressed in approximately *six years.* God is great. I am so extremely thankful to Jesus for this gift I never prayed for or expected, though others may have. The odd portion of any given day, I definitely can feel a bit down or sad like anyone may feel, but no depression. Thankfully the only medication I need is lithium for my bipolar disorder.

As Covid-19 hit our world with devastating loss and change, I was hyper-aware of the impact this could have on my mental health. There has been an incredible amount of unrest, fear and constant change. People losing family members, jobs, a sense of security, and peace. Personally, I had to teach in a completely different way using only technology via google hangouts with my students, teachers and administration. Suddenly, I was eighty percent administration/computer technician and twenty percent teacher. Technology and I are *not* best friends. Adding fuel to the fear of the unknown, was the horrible mass murder in Nova Scotia, the devastating floods in Fort McMurray, and even a smaller flood here in my small town of Lac La Biche. The news also highlighted horrible locust infestations in Africa and India, where many were already starving. Times such as these are extremely difficult and uncertain for everyone, especially somebody with a mental health disorder; it sounds like a perfect opportunity for depression to set in.

Gratefully, for me, it didn't. I admit feeling overwhelmed and uncertain. I felt angry and questioned God often. However, I armoured myself with the bible, memorizing scriptures and songs. It has been close to nine months in Western Canada dealing with Coronavirus. I am adjusting like everyone, sometimes daily, but I am not *consumed* by the idea of the illness and the precautions we must take.

I have not been depressed for even an entire day during the pandemic. This is incredible to me and speaks of the armour of God. The closer I keep to Him through scripture, songs and friends, the less likely Satan will take control of my thoughts and fears. I sought Him and He taught me, once again, to trust in Him.

"Come to me, all of you who are weary and burdened, and I will give you rest. Take my yoke upon you and learn from me, for I am gentle and humble in heart, and you will find rest for your souls." (Matthew 11:28-29) NIV

Chapter 3

INCURABLE

When getting any diagnosis, nobody wants to hear the word incurable. It is nasty, scary and sounds very much like a dead end filled with defeat, sorrow, and possible death. Sadly, this was exactly the prognosis my six year old daughter Kristy was given many years ago when diagnosed with Celiac disease. We were on my bed reading a new pamphlet that entailed symptoms, cautions and realities of the disease. When I read there is no cure, we both started crying. I took her in my arms and wept with her. I didn't want my daughter dealing with this limiting and difficult digestive disorder for her entire life.

Months before the diagnosis, Kristy was dealing with a lot of headaches, discomfort in her stomach and feelings of agitation more often. Her symptoms were progressing. One day I drove home from school to quickly pick up my children and get to an appointment for our passport photos and I found Kristy laying on her bed in a darkened room. When I asked her what was wrong, she replied, "The construction workers are pounding on my brain. It hurts so much mommy." Because of her history with headaches at the time, I comforted her and got her a cold glass of water and some ibuprofen. When I asked if she felt okay to go to our appointment, she felt she was. So, off we went in the van, when suddenly Kristy vomited all over the car! Guilt set in because I instinctively knew I never should have taken her out that day. We all headed home, and I cleaned Kristy up and tucked her in bed.

The very next day I made an appointment with our family doctor. This was the beginning of figuring out the puzzle regarding Kristy's illness. We had no known history of Celiac in our family. Our doctor thought Kristy could possibly have Celiac, but sent us to a pediatrician in the city for a specialists' opinion. A couple of weeks later, it was confirmed that Kristy had Celiac disease with a strongly elevated anti-transglutaminase blood level.[1] Kristy's blood result was roughly 300x higher than the minimum required to be diagnosed with Celiac. With these high levels, we realized we had

---

[1] According to TTGA Mayo Clinic Laboratories any blood level over 10.00U/ml indicates Celiac disease. Kristy's blood result was 323.1 U/ml

to make some extreme and immediate changes in her life, mainly with her food.

We started Kristy on a gluten free diet at a time when there was not very much available in our small town. It has improved a great deal since then. We shopped at a store called Kinnikinnick Foods in Edmonton and soon realized they also delivered, which was a Godsend. As she adjusted to new foods, different tastes and being very careful with what she was eating, I adjusted to cooking and preparing in a much different manner. Kristy often ate her own food while I prepared a similar meal for the rest of my family due to the extreme cost of gluten free food. Kristy had her own toaster, because even a crumb could cause a reaction in someone with this disease. Kristy's teachers knew about her new diagnosis and were very accommodating at school. We were all very careful. I tried to help Kristy focus on the positive side of her new eating lifestyle. It was fun to sit together and talk about all of the wonderful food she *could* still have.

However, mistakes were sometimes made and poor Kristy had to pay the consequences with horrible migraine-like headaches, bloating, and uncomfortable feelings in her stomach. I always kept Kristy's extra pancakes in a container in the fridge. One morning during her grade four year, we were finishing up breakfast when suddenly, to my horror, I realized I gave Kristy the wrong pancakes for breakfast! I was beyond words as I knew a small crumb could hurt her terribly; what would two whole pancakes do? I hugged her, apologized profusely, and we awaited the inevitable. I sent her on to school for the morning as often a reaction can take up to 5 hours and she was feeling completely fine at the time—other than the fact her mom just poisoned her. At 10:30am, I got the phone call from her school. I quickly got coverage and went to her rescue...finding her in a bathroom stall. She had been sick a few times already. I took her home and let her rest for the remainder of the day.

After this incident, we took even more precautions at home, but every once in a while she would still react to something. It was really hard to see our child suffer and for her to always feel so different. Birthday parties were probably the very hardest thing for her at the time. However, many parents made special accommodations for Kristy when she attended these affairs. I also knew other children were dealing with life-threatening things and I understood her diagnosis could have been much worse. My church family and prayer were my sanity at this tremendously trying time in my life. God comforted me, listened to me, led me and reminded me to forgive myself for the mistakes I made during these years.

A couple of years after the pancake fiasco, we headed to Cold Lake on a shopping trip and went for lunch in a neat restaurant by the marina called

Clarke's Eatery. After reading the menu, I realized, as I often did, there was very little Kristy would be able to have, so I decided to let her have a banana split. While not the healthiest option, there were few choices and the sundae brought a smile to Kristy's face. As she finished the sundae she asked me, "What do you think the crunchy part is mom?" It turned out that the "crunchy part" was a waffle cone. A waffle cone is most definitely made from wheat flour! We couldn't take back what Kristy had already eaten, so we again awaited the inevitable reaction. Five hours later...nothing. Seven hours later...nothing. Finally, Kristy headed off to bed and I expected to be woken by her with pain and a headache, but I wasn't! Kristy slept peacefully through the night and had absolutely no reaction. Two other very similar circumstances happened the summer of her twelfth year. In both of these situations, Kristy did not react to the wheat gluten she had ingested, so I felt it was time to have another blood test.

Amazingly, a couple of weeks later, Kristy's results from the blood test came back to reveal normal levels of anti-transglutaminase. She was cured from Celiac! God is good! We were ecstatic. Pizza was on the menu for dinner and I warned Kristy to take it easy at first. However, after six years of having to avoid normal bread products, she had two pieces of pizza and she was absolutely fine. We were so incredibly happy for our daughter.

How could this be? How could she be cured when this condition was incurable? Why did God grant us this miracle? I often prayed for her to be careful, to accept her new diet and for God to help her along the way in her new lifestyle. Intense praying was a given when she was having a reaction, but I honestly don't recall praying for an actual *cure* for Kristy. I was reading documented literature from credible doctors telling me this was a lifelong disease. I didn't think a cure was possible, but now I realize that *all* things are possible with God.

> **"Now to him who is able to do immeasurably more than all we ask or imagine, according to his power that is at work within us." (Ephesians 3:20) NIV**

Jesus healed our little girl. It is now seven years later and Kristy enjoys a wide variety of food, including food containing gluten. She sometimes chooses to limit her gluten intake, but she has not had one celiac episode since she was twelve years old. She is a very healthy, smart, faithful, kind and beautiful young lady who is now in her second year of nursing. We thank God regularly for this miracle!

Chapter 4

FAITH THROUGH THE FIRE

"Grief is raw, it tightens your chest like a vice and takes your breath away."

Crystal Cardinal

The following story was written from the heart of my very close friend Crystal. It is about an intense struggle she and her husband endured attempting to establish their family. The couple were married in the gorgeous area of Waterton, Alberta. My family was blessed to attend the wedding, and our pastor at the time travelled many miles to marry our two beautiful friends. The day was sunny and bright. The wedding was outdoors and *incredibly* beautiful. The ceremony was wonderful and everybody present enjoyed celebrating what a marriage ceremony is all about: a beautiful couple stating their love for one another publicly, under God's blessing. The beginning of amazing things to come! God most certainly blessed their marriage. They have grown into an ideal partnership of faithfulness, love, kindness and beauty. Nevertheless, Grant and Crystal have also endured pain and hardship in their marriage.

A couple of years after marrying, they realized they could not have children. Understandably, they were devastated. Their emotional response was comparable to experiencing a miscarriage. The couple were only able to discuss other possibilities after a time of grieving this news.

We waited years for a baby. We decided on the adoption route early on, yet still struggled to fill out the paperwork and jump through all the necessary bureaucratic hoops. The process was overwhelming to us.

Step 1-decide to adopt

Step 2-find a Christian adoption agency

Step 3-fill out a million forms

Step 4- get intervention checks done, criminal record checks completed

Step 5- get a house inspection & interview done

Step 6- find three references not related to you to write letters on your behalf

We stalled out here. Did we really want to do this? It may have even taken us a year to fill out those forms. Then, we found out each year we had to pay more money to stay in the pile of couples waiting to adopt! Each year the forms needed to be filled out...again. At times it seemed endless and hopeless.

The agency told us to add more pictures of ourselves in our photo album. We made four different albums throughout the years. We found marketing ourselves this way so strange. These thoughts prevailed: Does this picture make us look loving and caring? Are there too many pictures of holiday trips? Do we need more pictures of our friends' kids with us? We just wanted a child of our own...

By the end we nailed it and could now help anyone make a book to market themselves as a loving couple awaiting their forever family!

After a few years of waiting, wondering, heartache and confusion, out of the blue we got a phone call in the month of June. Is this it? Whoa!! We weren't sure *this* would ever happen. A part of us had given up and decided it wasn't God's plan. After the call, we met the birth mom at a pregnancy center. This was unusual for the agency but the mom was a Somalian from a Muslim family. Somehow we gained an understanding that this birth out of wedlock could mean something sinister and scary like an honor killing in her culture. She knew that she couldn't keep this baby and nobody in her family had found out about her pregnancy.

The day arrived. The birth mom posed for a picture with us in her hospital room after handing me her baby. She had to get back home before anyone noticed. It was surreal for us and I'm sure it was for her too. Pretty soon we were left alone in a room with this baby. Learning how to hold this beautiful baby girl and feed her and burp her and change her was *incredible*. Boom, just like that we had our child! I asked God to help me to love her as He does. He did. We gained confidence. I remember that beautiful black glistening hair that turned into these amazing ringlets when you got it wet, the likes of which I'd never seen before.

We had so many friends visit us and bring us presents. The agency said to isolate ourselves for the ten days the birth mom had to change her mind. However, we figured our situation was different because this mom couldn't keep her baby due to the cultural risk.

My neighbour was here when I got the phone call. My husband was at work. I couldn't *believe* she wanted her baby back. Our agency lady Kathy was telling me we had to bring the baby back to the city. I was shocked! Grant came home from work. My friends came and helped out. I was done. I was out. I'm not holding her or looking at her ever again. Shelley spent the night in the basement with the baby. I don't know how we could have gotten through that last night without her. Grant and I cried in our bed. I have no idea if we slept. I'd rather not revisit these feelings again, but I'll try.

My childhood best friend called and ordered me to pick her up and give her a proper goodbye or I would regret it for the rest of my *life*. She's still one of the only people who can order me to do something. It took all of my strength to pick her up, I asked God to help me and somehow I did it through blinding tears and feeling like I'd been gut-punched. I hope I never have to go through something that hard ever again. To date, this was the toughest thing I've lived through. Picking her up was like piercing my heart with blinding pain. Grant's sister came with us and our pastor followed us with his wife in their car all the way to the city to return her. I had no tears left to cry. I held her hand and she wrapped her hand around one of my fingers for most of the drive while I prayed. I prayed that something would happen and we'd get to keep her. I prayed for her and for us...prayed, prayed, prayed. Now, I can say thank-you God for surrounding us with loving friends and family who carried us through.

Looking back on it, it's weird that my closest

family members didn't get to meet her. My mom and cousin, the latter who is basically like my sister, were gone on a trip to Portugal. My dad was going to visit right away, but didn't make it until after she was gone.

My pastor's wife hugged me and said that wasn't your forever baby.

Why did God allow this to happen? Who knows? How many people ask this question every day as they cope with tragedies in their lives? Maybe just by going through this, it saved the birth mom and the baby's life because the birth mom's father realized other people now knew of the baby's existence. We'll never know. I know her birth mom loved her and she had so many Christians praying for her that she wouldn't have otherwise had. As for us, I do know one reason why this happened. It made us realize how badly we wanted to become parents. Up until that point, we were unsure if this road was one we truly wanted to travel down. After experiencing six days of parenthood, we now knew we wanted it more than *anything*.

I have flashbacks of all the people who grieved with us and had our backs throughout it all. That, I'll never forget and I am extremely grateful for. People from church that let me know they were praying for us. Pregnant friends who didn't want to be too overzealous in front of me. It was really sweet actually—you didn't need to mute your feelings. I could still share in your joy and it didn't increase my pain. My pain was always...just...*there*.

People told us, "This happened to friends of ours, they lost a baby or miscarried—blah, blah, blah—and then a couple months later they got pregnant or had a baby *immediately.*" Yes, isn't that great for your friends! Well it turns out that's not how it worked for us.

Trusting God was hard at this time. Why would He put it on our hearts to be parents and then not give us a baby?

So many close calls in the next year, I don't even know if I can remember them all.

One young birth mom we met, I just kept thinking, why can't she keep her baby? She was such a sweet person and already loved and named 'Liam' in utero. Well, she did end up keeping him after choosing us, but that one didn't sit well with me anyways. I remember her turning to us and looking us in the eyes and saying that the Holy Spirit gave her a feeling of complete peace over seeing our adoption photobook. This nugget of hope gave me enough to hang onto for the next few failed attempts at adoption. Looking back on it, these failed adoptions encouraged us to *keep* trying. Something was happening, but man it was a rollercoaster of emotions. It was a very long wait.

We waited all day for a phone call one time as a birth mom was in prison and trying to choose between us and another couple. Basically, if we ended up getting a phone call, we had to rush to pick up a baby, if not, then we weren't the couple she chose. She didn't even have time to meet a couple before giving birth.

Another phone call we got was a birth mom who ended up having drug problems. As the delivery date quickly approached, more and more of the truth came out that she ingested a larger amount of drugs than previously declared. We were so close to picking up this baby after she chose us (we never met her either), but the Holy Spirit was saying no. So many dead ends! I was beginning to give up.

I started my school year off like this: "Hi you're teaching my granddaughter this year. I'm your husband's auntie. Who's keeping your baby girl for you while you're teaching?"

I whispered to her, "Oh we had to give her back to her birth mom." I felt so bad having to tell her, along with the fact she felt *so* bad for asking. I was amazed in our small town that there were still people who hadn't heard our awful news.

By the end of the school year, after all of these false positives, I needed a break. After 15 years of teaching I applied for a personal leave and decided my mom and I would teach English overseas for a while as I needed time to reset and reflect on my life. I hit the pause button. At the time I didn't realize that Grant hadn't quite made the call to remove our file from the agency. *C'est la vie.*

I filled in for a maternity leave teaching position in Kindergarten after having applied for a leave in the fall. I taught for three months. Mom and I left for Costa Rica after deciding we didn't actually want to teach English in Chile; we really just wanted a vacation.

During our *first* week of holidays in January, Grant called me to let me know that another birth mom had chosen us. *Seriously*? My attitude was externally, "I'm not coming home early. If this is meant to be then it'll work out." Grant agreed. I tried to not think about it, but of course, my mom overheard and started asking me questions. Internally, I was wondering, could this actually be it? Don't *think* about it. In the back of my mind, I was reflecting about how God has worked in my life, especially with the *big* things. If I wanted something, I would pray but nothing would happen. I eventually would get to a place where I would completely let it go...then God delivered!

So I came home after a three week holiday and a couple days later, Grant and I were racing down south to meet the birth mom. It was interesting when the agency said she didn't like to talk much. Well, we ended up feeling quite at ease with her right away. She asked questions, we asked questions, and we didn't feel like she was quiet at all, just easy to talk to. During the visit, I requested she not tell us if it was a boy or a girl. However, as we were leaving and saying goodbye at the restaurant, I asked if she could please just tell us the sex of the baby, with a crack in my voice to which I said to myself, *man I'm already invested.* She said it was a boy and I almost burst into tears. Still, I couldn't completely trust that this was it.

Being that she was due in only a couple of weeks after we met her, on the way home we brainstormed names and couldn't agree on *anything.* I remember praying and a name came to me, then I was looking up people with that name online. At that moment, Grant said, what about this name? I couldn't believe he said the name aloud that I'd been searching online for. That was it. Thank you God.

I'm so grateful for our birth mom. She is a perfect fit for us. We didn't need to worry about anything at the hospital. She met with the hospital staff and had everything arranged! She even had me in the delivery room for his birth. I text her regularly to ask her things like, "When did your kids crawl? Walk? Get teeth? Do they love Kraft Dinner too?"

She couldn't keep our babe because her last child had some severe needs and she knew it would be too hard to have him and a new baby as well. It was amazing because her family was in support of the adoption too. I can't imagine how hard it was for her to give him up, but I can tell she was determined and wanted to do it *right.* What a huge *sacrifice* to make. I think until you've been on her side of adoption, we really can't comprehend the mixed emotions and turmoil that come along with it.

Our little boy is now two and a half. We try to see our birth mom twice a year, although Covid-19 messed up the plan a bit this year. We send pictures, talk on the phone and text with his biological mom. Our little boy is healthy, smart and amazing. We love him more than anything else on earth!

Reflection:

As soon as I found out that we couldn't have kids, I was drawn to the idea of adoption. My Mom was opposed to the idea and really wanted us to go through in vitro to have our own biological child. Grant and I never felt content with that idea. Sometimes when God is calling you to do something it can be *confusing*. But we looked to him for direction even though some people couldn't understand it! We didn't go very far down the fertility path, we just knew it wasn't for us and we didn't have peace about it. I think initially when we signed up with our adoption agency, we weren't too stressed. We thought if it's God's plan it will work out if not, so be it.

After a couple years of nothing happening we just thought it was not meant to be. When we did get a placement with Eliana, we were thrilled and fell completely in love with her. Looking back, I can see that perhaps God wanted us to be more desperate, longing and ready for his gift. It's funny it took losing her along with all of that pain and heartache for God to show us what we really wanted. Around this time, I actually prayed that God would give me a desire for His will in my life, I just had no idea how *painful* it would be to discover. Losing her could have caused us to push God away, but instead it caused us to cling to him. We knew He was at the heart of this somehow, but we just didn't understand.

We just grieved and kept going on with life. In the beginning, after returning her, it was hard to do everyday tasks and function as a human being, so we chose to lean on God and he provided us with our amazing friends and family for support. We are so *grateful* for them. More than a year went by, and I was specifically praying for a baby before I turned 40. God didn't agree. He had his own timing for our parenting story to unfold. It wouldn't begin until I let go completely, giving it up to Him and deciding that maybe this adoption thing wasn't going to work out after all. Maybe going to another country and trying to adopt wasn't the way to go. I had been frantically searching for ways to adopt all over the world. It was in between the failed matches following Eliana when I completely let go and figured I'd be okay either way....and that's when God delivered.

I can look back on many important crossroads in my life and it's always the same. Let go and let God and he'll give you the desires of your heart. When we've given up, we're confused, devastated and angry, God is still working in our lives even when we can't feel it. He loves us and really does have a plan for our lives.

When I look at our little boy I think about how smoothly everything went with his birth including the amazing doctor and nurses. I consider how well we get along with his birth mom and totally trust her. I honestly feel like we were born to be the parents of our little boy and his addition to our lives has blessed us as well as our families and our friends. He's our living, breathing *miracle*.

> **"Every good and perfect gift is from above, coming down from the Father of the heavenly lights, who does not change like shifting shadows." (James 1:17) NIV**

∽◯

Truly their son is a beautiful, bright light in Crystal and Grant's lives as well as so many lives he has touched in our community. I love him so much. The dynamics of a small town mean many joyous occasions are shared together, but we also share our grief and pain. So many people in Lac La Biche wanted this beautiful couple to have a child. We were incredibly saddened by the loss of their first child and many questions arose out of the pain we shared.

"Why would God do this to them? How could this have happened? It seemed *so* perfect."

Yes, many tears were shed and hearts were broken over the loss our dear friends endured. Could this truly be God's plan? The rest of their story most definitely answers that question. When we can't see through the pain, we pray through the pain. I have come to realize it is very important to praise God in the pain and our most difficult circumstances. We must trust in Jesus. God asks us to be thankful in all things. *All* things means the tough, hard and ugly things included. In my life I have learned to cry out thanks in some of the most painful, most excruciating times, knowing the Saviour has a purpose in this pain. It is extremely hard at times. However, His plan is always best. The power and resulting effects of those most trusting prayers are reflected in so many areas of my life where God carried me through to a peaceful shore.

There are a couple of songs which I love that speak a great deal about the journey my friends went through. **"Thy Will be Done"** by Hillary Scott and **"Into the Sea"** by Tasha Layton are two examples.

MIRACLES UNFOLDING

I was inspired to write the following poem shortly after witnessing these two people I love so very much experience such incredible, polar opposite emotions in such a short period of time. It was so difficult to see Grant and Crystal go through such excruciating pain. It has also been incredible to see their hopeful story unfold.

Raw Emotion

Anticipation–wondering, excited, nervous, eager, longing, hoping, happy

Grateful Delivery – blessing, honor, glory, ecstatic, euphoric, sharing, inhaling the beauty, elated, answered prayer…LOVE!

Depressing Departure – horror, unbelief, insanity, fear, questioning, wretched crying, stabbing pouring pain…WHY?

Recovery – Slow emotion, hanging on with strings to faith, friends, family, prayer, Pastor, rainbows, flowers, sunshine, tears, screams, tears, questions… HOPE IN JESUS!

Chapter 5

CAR VS. BULL MOOSE

It was a cold, wintry evening on the night of December 8, 2018 when Dale, Jesse, his friend Omar and I headed out on the road to a small community just over an hour away for a hockey game. I had reservations about going that evening, especially because my son Jesse had been injured the week before and suffered a mild concussion. He felt he was healed enough to play, but as a mom, I had my doubts and I didn't think it was a good idea. In this particular year, Jesse was one of the top scorers on his team. Unfortunately, this often made him a target for some rough checks into the boards and the team we were playing was known to be extremely rough.

I tried to focus on God's great grace. I prayed for safe travel, "God please keep us all safe on the road this evening. Please do not allow anyone or anything to harm us, and please don't allow us to harm anyone or anything either. In Jesus name, I pray." This was the typical travel prayer we have said for years. It reminded me to rely on God for our safety and comforted me in our many travels.

Approximately forty-five minutes into our drive, my husband Dale made an odd comment and put his foot on the brakes. I looked up and was shocked to see an enormous bull moose standing across the road about forty feet in front of us! He wasn't moving and we *weren't* stopping. With these road conditions, I realized Dale would not be swerving into the ditch. In a desperate, terrified voice I cried out, "Jesus save us!"

We braced for impact and we hit the moose, bringing us from approximately 60-70 km/hr to a sudden stop within seconds. From here on my thoughts were a bit jumbled due to shock and the realities of what could have been. I realized we were still *alive* and there were no broken bones or major cuts, despite the windshield being completely smashed and the steering wheel bent in half. But, the most powerful revelation was that Jesus answered my frantic prayer and we were all saved!

From the back seat, Jesse witnessed the moose, back on his legs, wandering into the ditch toward the forest. Even the *moose* seemed okay. My travel prayer was also answered. God is *great*.

A truck pulled up behind us within a minute.

He checked out the scene and called 911. Another vehicle travelling the other direction quickly showed up and the kind Samaritan allowed us— moose hair, small amounts of blood, and all—into his vehicle for warmth. We were still in shock, but so grateful. Soon a variety of emergency vehicles were headed our way. They had sent more than the usual amount of assistance for a normal car accident as they heard the collision involved a small 2005 Corolla, four people and a bull moose. They actually didn't expect to find *any* survivors. They were thankfully surprised.

After the emergency medical technicians asked us a wide variety of questions about our physical health, they appeared confused. It was incredible to them there were no fatalities, but no injuries either? They asked some things more than once just to be sure.

Dale's small cuts were examined. He and I had a great deal of glass on our heads and faces so we headed into the emergency to get our eyes flushed, but that was it. The boys were completely fine, though shaken. Thank goodness and thanks be to God our son didn't have to witness what easily could have happened in the front seat of our small car.

A great deal of thanks was given to the emergency response team in Goodridge, Alberta. They were incredible. Showing professionalism, compassion and providing us a sense of comfort in the midst of the distress we were experiencing. They even allowed us to head to the fire hall for a more comfortable setting and snacks as we awaited our ride home. Their service went above and beyond expectations and we were truly grateful.

Coaches and other travellers came upon us soon after the accident. Thankfully, the hockey game was cancelled and Jesse didn't have to play with a possible concussion. God had a different plan.

Often when reflecting on this terrifying evening, I give thanks to God for this miracle. Is the miracle the fact that none of us were injured or killed in the accident in such a small car during winter conditions? Or, is the miracle the lengths God will go to protect His children? Was this humongous, beautiful animal sent to us as a gift? Did he block the road intentionally so we did not make it to the game?

When I prayed to Jesus for help, He answered immediately. As a Christian, I realize our prayers are not always answered in such short timing. Often we wait hours, days or even years for prayers to be answered. However, it is a beautiful thing to know that when I truly needed a prayer to be answered instantly, it *was*. A song that I love by Jesus Culture addresses this. "**Break Every Chain**" talks about power in the name of Jesus.

Once I was home after the accident, I was cleaning out my purse in the bathroom. There was so much moose hair and glass everywhere. I took a small receipt from my purse and wrapped up some of the moose hair like a present. On the receipt, I drew a cross. I carry this little gift of moose hair in my purse as a reminder of God's love for me and my family.

Again, the gratefulness we have for this miracle in our lives is beyond words. We have prayed many thankful prayers.

> **"Put on all the armour that God gives you, so that you will be able to stand up against the Devil's evil tricks." (Ephesians 6:11) GNB**

Spiritual warfare is real. The armour I possessed was my *faith* in Jesus when I called out to Him. Not only did He protect us in our vehicle, but I believe He wanted the game cancelled entirely that night. I truly believe God went through radical lengths to protect my injured son that evening. Who knows what Satan had planned?

Chapter 6

THE SKIN I'M IN

The next story may not seem like a miracle to many people, however, if you struggle with a condition called psoriasis you will feel differently! Psoriasis is a skin condition that causes skin to reproduce ten times faster than normal in certain areas. It can be all over the body and on the scalp or in areas around the knees, elbows and lower back. It is a very difficult disease with no cure, merely treatments and creams to help the symptoms.[2]

I started to get psoriasis around the age of 26. I had eczema when I was younger but I never had psoriasis. It started on my head along my hairline in the back. It can be very embarrassing, unsightly and uncomfortable to have psoriasis on the scalp. It is also tougher to treat because of our hair, and

---

[2] **"Psoriasis** is a common, long-term (chronic) disease with **no** cure." Mayo Clinic (1998-2020)

is often mistaken for dandruff. Soon the psoriasis moved to a few more areas on my body, mostly my legs and torso.

After a few years, my head cleared up but I was getting more spots on my body. My doctor was very knowledgeable and she prescribed various medications and offered many suggestions to ease the discomfort. Finally, after having tried every cream and ointment, moisturizing creams and a little bit of sun, we tried an injection. This anti-inflammatory injection is administered in the skin layer and it hurts a great deal! It was worth the pain as it did calm down the patches incredibly quickly. However, they would come back or another spot would emerge. This treatment couldn't be done very often due to the fact that the skin can become thin from the drug. Still, I was happy for some reprieve, and some hope it may improve.

In my late twenties, I moved to Lac La Biche and gave up on therapy. I continued with creams and ointments, prayer, some sunlight and considered an oral medication or biologic remedy. However, both of the latter treatments suppress the immune system, and being a teacher who was often ill due to many viruses being passed around, I decided against pursuing these.

There was some thought my psoriasis may have been influenced by my lithium medication. The timing would be about right to establish a connection between the two, as I had started on

Lithium regularly when I was about 20 and over a few years my body could have rebelled. Either way, I wasn't going to risk going off my medication which helps my mental health incredibly. I would have to accept, endure and educate myself.

I joined the Psoriasis Society to learn more and I supported them financially with their research in finding a cure. I was very saddened to hear of many situations where children were experiencing this disease in horrible ways. Some children and adults suffered with extreme psoriasis *all over* their bodies. Many were questioned about whether or not it was contagious and many were bullied because of their condition. The effects on a person can be incredibly debilitating and depressing. I prayed both individually and collectively for everybody dealing with psoriasis' horrible effects. Hearing others stories allowed me to put my own struggle into perspective.

Fast forward a few years…I was 30 and I found out I was expecting our first child. As my baby daughter was growing in my body, my psoriasis was clearing up. I was really excited. Unfortunately, it came back after I had finished nursing her. The same thing happened when I was expecting Kristy 3 years later. This healing was *wonder*ful and I hoped the disease would stay away. Sadly, this was not the case, and once again the plaques returned after I finished nursing.

The interesting thing about hormones is that

when I was expecting my son Jesse, my psoriasis did not clear up at all. I was now 37 years old and still dealing with this skin disease. Usually, it didn't bother me too much; luckily most of my psoriasis was covered by clothing the majority of the time. However, the flakiness, itchiness, bleeding, and constant creams and ointments did get trying on certain days. I shed quite a few tears because of this disease.

A few years later, Dale and I took a vacation to the Dominican Republic without the kids to reconnect and find some healing in God's beautiful creation. The resort we stayed at was amazing. The sun, surf, white sand and gorgeous turquoise water was incredible. Another purpose for going was for me to complete my first book. God allowed me time to finish most of my memoir at home with three young kids to take care of and a full time job, but I still had the most difficult portion of the book to complete. The Dominican couldn't have been in a more *perfect* setting to accomplish this.

My psoriasis-ridden skin was exposed and saw the sun for a good portion of the day, every day for two weeks. One original patch on my right thigh had been there for 18 years and it kept shrinking during our vacation. By the time the holiday was over, it had *totally* disappeared. I was extremely thankful and somewhat hopeful about the other patches too.

The area on my thigh *stayed* clear. Unfortunately

though, the other parts of my body affected by this disease were still very inflamed. I endured the creams, ointments and vitamin D tablets, and continued to pray for a cure for psoriasis.

Eight years later, I was 52 years old when I noticed the size of my spots were getting a little bit smaller. After a shower, one of my spots which I had for many, many years was healed. I was ecstatic! In a full length mirror a few months after this discovery, I looked in disbelief to see that my psoriasis had cleared up entirely. After having dealt with psoriasis for 26 years, I had no more...I was *cured*.

The only thing different in my life at this time was menopause and a medication called progesterone I was taking for a couple of years to assist with my sleeping patterns.

There is not supposed to be a cure for psoriasis. I was so extremely grateful for this miracle. *Jesus* is the cure. He allowed me to be healed. What a wonderful reason to celebrate and to be hopeful for others dealing with this dreaded disease.

"With God all things are Possible."
(Matthew 19:26) NIV

A song that also comes to mind when facing our many human struggles is **"The Eye of The Storm"** by Ryan Stevenson. It speaks of hope in all of our difficulties when we call on the *One* who is in control.

Chapter 7

JESSE'S HEALING

It was early January when my 16 year old son approached me with a mark on his skin. It didn't take me long to identify it as psoriasis. However, I didn't tell him at first. Our first "go-to" in our household with skin irritations is Vitamin E cream. I told him to apply it liberally and to keep an eye on the rash. A couple of days later, Jesse showed me another spot on his torso. This time I could see the red inflammation and the flakiness on top. I almost cried when I told him he needed to make an appointment with the doctor to get it assessed.

Jesse was very upset when the doctor confirmed my suspicion the spot was psoriasis. Knowing the many creams and ointments used for this condition merely help the symptoms but don't take the psoriasis away, we tried a different approach. I compounded a few suggested essential oils with coconut oil into an ointment for Jesse to try. We put it on the two spots a few different times, but unfortunately it didn't seem to make much difference. Thankfully, the spots didn't get any larger. At this time, we also decided to re-wash all of Jesse's clothes and bedding in a detergent without any perfumes or dyes. The next day, Jesse woke up with a rash *all over* his torso. His front and back were completely covered with red patches. We were in shock, fear and tears. After having come to the end of a 26 year battle with psoriasis, how could this be happening to my son?

Recalling what I had gone through with my psoriasis for so many years, the word alone really frightened Jesse. He knew psoriasis was long-term and usually incurable. Now, the rash was everywhere on his torso and he didn't know what to do. So, he looked up. Jesse gave this awful condition to God and asked for healing. He asked God to please take it all away.

My family and I were praying for Jesse's healing, and I was also attending a bible study every Wednesday during this time. At the end of each session, we always share who we would like the group to pray for. I asked our group to pray for Jesse's skin condition, explaining how it was affecting him psychologically as well as physically. He had started spending more time in his room and acting quite defeated.

Miraculously, by the end of February Jesse's

skin was *completely* healed. The red marks had disappeared entirely. Jesus heard Jesse's prayer, along with many others praying for him. We were so incredibly grateful for this miracle! What could have been a life-long condition, ended up lasting only two months. God is *good*. We remembered to give thanks.

Understandably, many people may wonder why Jesse suffered with psoriasis for only two months when I suffered with it for 26 years, and others for an entire lifetime. It is very hard for us to comprehend. God's timing is God's timing. However, I do believe in both situations, our healing came from prayer and faith. They were miracles from God. A song that speaks to this is called **"Confidence" b**y Sanctus Real. It speaks about God giving faith like Daniel, hope like Moses and a heart like David to help us face *giants* with confidence.

> *"Trust in the Lord with all your heart and lean not on your own understanding but in all ways submit to Him and He will make your paths straight."* **(Proverbs 3:5-6) NIV**

Jesus performed a similar miracle almost 2000 years ago for a man a suffering from a skin disease:

Jesus Heals a Man

When Jesus came down from the hill, large crowds followed him. Then a man suffering from a dreaded skin disease came to him, knelt down before him, and said, "Sir, if you want to, you can make me clean."Jesus stretched out his hand and touched him. "I do want to," the man answered. "Be clean!" At once the man was healed of his disease. Then Jesus said to him, "Listen! Don't tell anyone, but go straight to the priest and let him examine you; then in order to prove to everyone that you are cured, offer the sacrifice that Moses ordered." **(Matthew 8:1-4) GNB**

Due to this dreaded skin disease, the man had probably been isolated from others and possibly embarrassed. He was likely feeling hopeless about this disease in his life. He may not have been able to work. Suddenly, he heard about Jesus and all he had been doing to heal others. He knew Jesus could save him, but he wasn't sure if Jesus wanted to. He called out to Jesus and was *cured*. I imagine his gratitude went beyond measure. Jesse and I are also *extremely* grateful to God for our healing.

Chapter 8

MIRACLES UNFOLDING

Peace is what I feel most strongly in my life since I have come to know and trust in the Lord. I have been blessed with an abundance of gifts. I have been blessed with an abundance of miracles. In allowing Jesus to take the wheel as the captain of my ship, He has allowed me to reflect on many miracles that happened in my life even before I was a believer. God's grace is *incredible*.

When considering some of the specific miracles Jesus performed while here on earth, I can truly be grateful in knowing that He lives today. We serve a living God in the form of the Holy Spirit. He works through our faith in Him.

Some of the miracles I have witnessed in my life mirror the miracles Jesus performed almost *two thousand years ago.* I was so mentally ill in my late teens and early twenties, and so deeply depressed and distraught, I believed a monster was inside me. Was this monster a demon like those spoken of in biblical times? At that time in my life, my sinful nature and distance from Jesus would have created a large opening for Satan to enter my heart and mind.

In the New Testament, Jesus hears a mother's cry to heal her daughter from a demon. This Canaanite woman saw Jesus walking with His disciples in the area where she lived. She was desperate for his healing because her daughter had a demon and she was in horrible condition. At first, Jesus hesitated and the disciples asked him to ignore her as she was making so much noise. However, the lady proved her faith in Jesus and while she was speaking with him, her daughter was healed immediately! (Matthew 15:21-28).

Jesus heard *my* mother's cry too. The love shown to me by my family during that tumultuous time, was most definitely healing and essential in allowing me to dig myself out of the darkness after my attempted suicide. Their love worked like an arrow in my heart, redirecting me upward to our Heavenly Father. Healing was not as instantaneous as the example in the bible, but my healing and my mental health turned completely around in an amazing unfolding of faith, hope and love.

Again the bible tells us, Jesus performed another miracle of healing skin disorders for a group of men:

A parallel to having strong faith and giving thanks comes in another miracle performed by Jesus in his life here on earth. Jesus was on his way to Jerusalem through the border of Samaria and Galilee. He was at the entrance to a village when he saw ten men suffering from a dreaded skin disease. They shouted at Jesus to take pity and cure their condition. Jesus asked them to go to the priest to be examined. As they walked in that direction, Jesus *healed* their skin. Later, only one of the ten came back to give thanks to Jesus. Jesus asked where the others were. Then, he said to this man, "Get up and go; your faith has made you well." (Luke 17:11-19) GNB

Similarly to these men, after suffering over a long period of time my *incurable* psoriasis became *curable* for Jesus. I am incredibly grateful. I have given thanks many times.

Strong faith and losing faith are both exemplified in the miracle when Jesus walks on water and calls out to Peter. Peter came onto the water and was actually walking toward Jesus. Such amazing faith and an astounding miracle.

However, as the water became a bit rough, Peter lost his faith in Jesus' ability to hold him close and Peter started to sink.

I have never walked on water, but I have most definitely gone through periods of strong, unsinkable faith along with times of uncertainty and doubt as a believer. When the waters get turbulent and times become tough, this is when we need to call out to God even more. God wants us to depend on Him in all things. I have learned to praise God in the storms, believing in His power and purpose in my struggles. As in Peter's example, Jesus is right there and ready to pull us to safety or allow us to feel His peace in the waiting. Many of you may have read the anonymous poem called *Footprints in the Sand*. In this poem, a man has a dream in which he looks back on his life and realizes at the most troubled times, there was only one set of footprints, instead of two. When he questions why he had to walk alone through the hardest times, God responds: "It was then that I carried you." God carries us through, even when we don't notice Him. He carries us when we need Him most. He *loves* us.

"It was then that I carried you."

A song that I often listen to related to learning to trust completely is by Jason Gray entitled, "**I'm Gonna Let it Go**".

Are you feeling burdened and in need of "letting go" of a few things in your life? You can trust that God has got this. He will guide your journey, if you allow Him to.

Chapter 9

MIRACLES AND YOU

When considering miracles in your life, there will always be a different perspective depending on where you are with your faith in Jesus. You may be a believer experiencing miracles unfolding in your life with great reverence. Or possibly, you are a believer who hasn't really contemplated the amazing happenings in your life as miracles from above. If you are not yet a believer, you may feel certain things occurred in your life were "lucky coincidences." Finally, you may not yet be a believer and feel no miracle could ever happen to *you*. Perhaps you have made too many mistakes. You sin too often.

The true miracle and transformation comes in believing in a living God. The power of Jesus is incredible and it starts with the beautiful forgiveness of our confessed sins along with a relationship with Him. He loves us more than anything we could ever imagine. The lovely song "No Matter What" by Ryan Stevenson reinforces **that no matter what we've done we can't erase His amazing love for us.**

If you are not a believer, or feel you don't have a relationship with Jesus, it is not too late to give your life to Christ, confess your sin and ask Him into your heart forever. He hears us at any age. He knows our hearts.

The short stories I've shared are incredible examples of God's faithfulness and love. This is a relationship that I would *never* give up. Though I am uniquely made and loved by God, I am an average person. I am just a woman, a sinner, who has suffered in complete and utter darkness and was eventually led into a beautiful, peaceful light— the light and hope of Jesus!

He continues to bless my life daily. Does this mean the lives of Christians are easy and free from trouble? On the contrary, Christians are not promised a life free from strife. Instead, we are promised eternal life after death and assured God is always with us in our struggles, confessions and battles. We are not alone.

In the last few years, since I wrote my first book, I have experienced many struggles and heartaches. Dale had his second hernia operation and needed to be off work for a couple of months. His healing was slow but steady. My sister had a hysterectomy result in terrible complications. Her bowel was nicked, she endured many surgeries, and came very close to losing her life. My aunt had a heart attack leaving plaque in her brain. Her recovery was incredible but her left leg still has nerve damage. On a holiday in Europe with my girls, I was informed my dad was in the hospital with heart complications. I felt extremely helpless being so far away. The only thing I could do was pray, and I did. My dad ended up having a heart operation about 10 days later as he needed to be monitored in the hospital for a blood complication. I made it home for the operation. He underwent a double bypass and a valve replacement. His heart is as good as *new*. Then, a couple of years ago I lost a very special lady to Alzheimer's. It was extremely difficult to see her in a shell of herself for so long before she passed. It was so hard to lose her. I still get very sad thinking about her suffering and how much I miss her.

On top of these personal trials, all of us can relate to the multitude of struggles 2020 brought. Difficulties and heartaches are universal when we think about the effects of Covid-19 and also things such as floods, tornadoes, locusts and fires. These types of situations can manifest in a great deal of stress and anxiety. The uncertainty of life can leave us feeling stretched to the limit. There are universal disasters and diseases affecting all of us.

Yet, despite all of this chaos and instability, Jesus can teach us to live a life filled with joy and hope.

No, being a Christian doesn't take our struggles away. However, it does allow us to let go of our trials and give them to the One who can heal, comfort, love and direct us. Again, I've learned to praise God in the storms. He is the constant from the beginning of time into eternity. I am so very grateful for His daily presence in my life.

We have found a wonderful church family and incredible friends here in Lac La Biche. Dale and I have been blessed with good, solid jobs while living here. I have taught so many amazing children and met wonderful parents. We have brought up three beautiful children in this small town. We are filled with gratitude for the gifts God has given us.

As my faith continues to grow, I would like to share some things I've learned about maintaining a relationship with Jesus. I always pray. I pray in my head, out loud, with others, through song and sometimes on my knees. I attend church regularly. I read God's word often. I have attended bible studies which have helped grow my faith. I watch episodes based on bible teachings from RightNow Media. Finally, I walk and talk a great deal with my Christian friends. I have learned to give more of myself in time, friendships, church ministries, and monetarily to church and other charities. I am constantly reminded how true it is that *to give is to receive*.

My faithful lifestyle may sound a bit overwhelming to some...believe me, my Christian journey didn't start with all of this. I actually started with a desire to have my children know God and for our marriage to prosper. Soon we found a wonderful church and the rest God has grown from there.

God's story is so very relevant today and every day. The bible is *His* story—history! The bible is also present and future. Jesus is everlasting to everlasting, therefore His story never goes out of style. We can learn about how and why God wants us to live to worship Him. Peace and hope beyond understanding is our reward. Approximately **800** years before Jesus' birth, this God-breathed word was shared through the prophet, Isaiah:

> **For to us a child is born, to us a son is given, and the government will be on his shoulders. And he will be called Wonderful Counselor, Mighty God, Everlasting Father, Prince of Peace. (Isaiah 9:6) NIV**

Good deeds will flow from our love and trust in Jesus. However, it is *not* true that if we merely do enough good works God will accept us into heaven. Once you call out to Him to be your saviour and confess your sins you are saved. You will feel the pull to do good as you are becoming closer to God and more like Jesus.

Our own personal ships can be old, breaking apart, have holes and often seem to be in extremely rough water. But we are not meant to sail alone. If you haven't already, call out to Jesus to be the captain of *your* ship, the way it was always meant to be. It is a conscious, daily choice to be a believer. Our creator loves every one of us so very much! He is waiting at your porthole...just invite Him in. You truly have eternal life waiting for you in heaven and beautiful internal peace while here on earth. The opposite is true for those who don't know the Lord, who don't confess their sins and who don't commit their lives to Him before they pass. The opposite is truly hell.

> **Jesus answered him, "I am the way, the truth, and the life; no one goes to the Father except by me..." (John 14:6) GNB**

As you walk through the doors of my church, this Scripture written in very large font welcomes all who enter:

> **"Come to me, all you who are weary and burdened, and I will give you rest. Take my yoke upon you and learn from me, for I am gentle and**

humble in heart, and you will find rest for your souls." (Matthew 11:28-29) NIV

We need our Creator! He is our guide to love, light, hope, peace and joy. He is our compass, anchor and fortress. He is our salvation. He is our miracle giver. One verse I repeatedly turned to during the initial change and anxiety caused by the Covid-19 pandemic was from the book of Philippians:

> **Do not be anxious about anything, but in every situation, by prayer and petition, with thanksgiving, present your requests to God. And the peace of God, which transcends all understanding will guard your hearts and your minds in Christ Jesus. (Philippians 4:6-7) NIV**

Oh how these words have been a comfort to me during such a *tumultuous* time. Life here on earth is fleeting. We only have so much time on this platform. Our trust in the Lord leads to salvation. This salvation is not inherited from our parents or grandparents. It depends on our personal relationship with Jesus. There is a beautiful heaven awaiting us so we may live eternally free from pain, tears, physical constraints, financial constraints, pandemics and war. Can you imagine streets paved with gold and not potholes or litter? Imagine feeling love, hope and peace instead of fear. It can start *today*.

In the biblical examples of Jesus performing miracles, every miracle was accompanied by faith. I certainly maintained *great* faith as I personally experienced the love and healing of our Savior. I am extremely grateful for the miracles I have been part of either directly or indirectly in my life. Though these are wonderful, they do not define my faith. I am not expecting or desiring miracles to happen in my life. On the contrary, I am merely incredibly thankful and my faith does not depend on miracles. If God decides, or does not decide to perform any more miracles in my life or the lives of others whom I love, my faith remains. He is the constant. My faith is anchored in God's truth. The miracles are a *blessing*.

Nothing will ever fill the cup of contentment like the love of Jesus. Many people seek to fill voids in their lives with unhealthy relationships, food, alcohol, drugs, lust, purchasing, extreme exercise…I could go on and on. I know because I was one of them, but now I am fulfilled and at peace. I am loved and I love others. This amazing grace and life can be yours too, if it is not already... it is a truly *miraculous* relationship!

Printed in the United States
by Baker & Taylor Publisher Services